Pla   Retirement

by

Alison Mitchell

P
PROFILE BOOKS

First published in Great Britain in 2001 by
Profile Books Ltd
58A Hatton Garden
London EC1N 8LX
www.profilebooks.co.uk

Copyright © Alison Mitchell, 2001

Typeset in Melior by MacGuru
info@macguru.org.uk

Printed and bound in Great Britain by
Bookmarque, Croydon, Surrey

A CIP catalogue record for this book is available from the British Library.

ISBN 1 86197 335 7

Contents

Introduction

Retirement – that time in your life when you can really start to live. Free from the shackles of work, deadlines, commuting and lack of time, you can start to live your dreams. You might want to travel, study, take up new interests or get stuck into hobbies you already have.

More of us are opting for early retirement and, with advances in medicine and healthcare and improvements in general living standards, we can now realistically expect a good 20 years before age starts to slow us down.

But there is a price to pay for this. A generation or so ago, people joined the workforce in their late teens and worked on till age 60 or 65, and healthy retirement often lasted not much more than a decade.

Nowadays, millions of people are in their early 20s by the time they finish their university or college course and start a job. Many of them will hope to retire at 55, and then have 2–3 decades of active years.

So we've moved in a fairly short time span from having 40 years of working life to pay for 10–15 years of retirement, to having 30 years of working life to pay for 30 years or more of retirement. And these sums won't add up for many people. There is just not enough time while you are working to pay for the sort of retirement you might want.

The golden years won't have much of a sparkle without a decent pot of gold to go with them. No matter how glamorous or modest you expect your lifestyle to be, you'll need an income to support it.

That's what this book is all about. It will guide you through your first plan, so that you can work out just how much you will need to live on, match your investments with the amount of risk you are prepared to take with your money, check out your pension, your tax, your health plans and your home. And when the time comes to trade in your alarm clock, this book will make sure that you are making the best of the pension fund you've saved.

All the costs and figures are correct for the tax year 2000/01. Most tax allowances and benefits change at the beginning of the new tax year, which starts on 6th April 2001, so if you are unsure of exact figures in subsequent years, it's worth checking them out. Use www.open.gov.uk for government departments and the Inland Revenue.

The golden rule is to plan ahead for your retirement. And the platinum rule is do it little and often. Providing you start early enough, and save regularly, you should be in clover. But even if you have left it late, or don't have much to put by, there's plenty you can do to make the best of what you have got. And it may be more than you think.

For many people earning serious money begins in their 40s, when couples often start to have two incomes coming into the family home again. By their 50s the mortgage may be almost repaid and the expense of funding a growing family starting to tail off.

By the time you reach retirement the picture is even brighter. Stopping work doesn't have to mean the start of scrimping and saving. Make the right moves now and you'll be set up for a happy and wealthy retirement.

2 Planning ahead

⇨ **How much will you need to retire on – work it out**
⇨ **A pension isn't your only option**

It's a simple concept really – the earlier you start to save for your retirement, the more you will have in your pot when you get there. There are two reasons for this:
- You will be saving for more years
- The money will have longer to grow.

So the chances are, if you start to fund a pension while you are in your 20s you will have a decent sized pot of money when you hit 60. Leave it till you are in your 30s or 40s and you will have to save much more.

And the figures are staggering.

Someone wanting to retire at 65 on £20,000 a year at today's prices – that's just over £1,500 a month – will have to put substantial amounts of money into a pension fund. The cost will take your breath away. Assuming they are starting from scratch the savings needed are:

A man	
Age 25	£350 a month
Age 30	£550 a month
Age 40	£850 a month

A woman	
Age 25	£440 a month
Age 30	£530 a month
Age 40	£830 a month

That's a huge amount of money to save every month – particularly if you remember that for many people 40 doesn't seem that old to be starting a pension.

The problem is that very few of us sit down, work out how much we think we'll need at retirement and then calculate how much we should put into a pension to get to that figure. If we have a pension at all, it's usually based on what we can afford to put into it, or what our employer expects us to pay, and then we just hope that it will be enough. Crossed fingers and a head in the sand attitude are not much good at boosting the size of a pension fund though.

So it's important to do the calculation.

What sort of lifestyle do I want in my retirement?

The first thing to do is look at the lifestyle of your parents or their friends who have already retired. Who has the sort of life that you might want? Will you want to do a lot of travelling abroad – and flying in business class perhaps because you prefer the extra comfort and will be prepared to pay for it? Will you still need two cars, including a large comfortable one? What about your house, will you still want the family home? Will you be trading down to a bungalow and using some of the money from your house to fund your old age?

You don't need to know to the last detail the sort of life you'll want in your retirement, but try to paint a general picture and work out from that what you think it will cost you in today's money.

Could you sustain your chosen lifestyle now on £20,000 a year, or £30,000 … or maybe you'll only need £15,000?

Most people wanting a comfortable, but not necessarily luxurious, life in retirement would manage on 65–75% of their final salary.

Expert tip: **An under-funded pension can almost be worse than no pension at all because it lulls you into a false sense of financial security. It is crucial to calculate what sort of lifestyle you will get from the money you are currently saving.**

Once you know how much you might need every year, it's possible to work out how much you should be putting aside every month of your working life.

Most of the large pension providers, banks, financial advisers and financial websites will be able to do a proper calculation for you – based on your individual figures, age and tax position. But the figures below will give you some idea of the size of the money mountain you are about to scale.

Someone earning £30,000 a year wants to retire at age 60 on 75% of their salary – which would give them £1,875 a month in today's money. The savings required if starting from scratch are:

A man	
Age 25	£600 a month
Age 30	£740 a month
Age 40	£1,240 a month

	A woman
Age 25	£680 a month
Age 30	£840 a month
Age 40	£1,400 a month

If they decided to retire at 55 they would need to save much more:

	A man
Age 25	£850 a month
Age 30	£1,070 a month
Age 40	£1,980 a month

	A woman
Age 25	£930 a month
Age 30	£1,180 a month
Age 40	£2,190 a month

Very, very few of us are paying that sort of money into our pension fund. So we will have to either scale down our spending in retirement or fund our old age in another way.

How to boost your pension fund

There are several ways of plumping up your funds so that you have enough in retirement.

The options are:
- Your pension
- Investments
- Your home
- Leaving it till later
- Part-time work.

Your pension

The problem with pensions is that they are seldom at the top of our financial priorities. In our 20s and 30s retirement seems a long way off. There are more pressing needs for our salary so there is rarely enough left over to pay as much as we would like into a pension. You can leave it till later and try to make up lost ground, but that will cost you a lot more. For full details on topping up see Chapter 3.

Don't forget the state pension, currently worth around £3,500 a year. It would be difficult to live just on that – as many of today's pensioners are finding – but remember to add the figure into your calculations.

There are some changes being made to the way state pensions are paid which could affect you.

- SERPs, the earnings related top-up that some employees will be entitled to, is being phased out and will be replaced in April 2002 by the State Second Pension.
- Women's state retirement age is being pushed back. In the decade 2010–20 the retirement age for women will move from age 60 to age 65, so they won't get the state pension until later than they might expect.
- Stakeholder pensions are being introduced in April 2001 (see Chapter 3 for full details).
- Minimum Income Guarantee has been introduced which provides a means-tested safety net for those retiring with little or no income or savings. It means that the poorest pensioners will be guaranteed a minimum income. In effect, the state pension will be topped up for those with very little else. It's currently worth £78.45 for single pensioners and £121.95 for married couples (2000/01), though it will rise as the years go on, probably reaching

£100 a week for a single pensioner and £150 a week for a pensioner couple by 2003.

Investments

By the time you hit retirement you should have some capital built up in savings accounts, or in tax-free plans such as ISAs, PEPs or TESSAs, or unit or investment trusts. This will all be money that you can use to top up your pension, either by spending part of the lump sum or by living off the income. For full details on how to make the most of any money you have, see Chapter 4.

Your home

Many of us have as much money tied up in our home as we do in our pension fund. Give some thought to where you will live when you retire. Staying put will mean that you are locking up this capital and, if your house is a large one, you will have to pay the bills that go with it. If you intend to sell up and move to a smaller house or flat you will release some of your funds and, hopefully, cut the cost of many of the bills. The housing options are fully explored in Chapter 9.

Cash saver: **Remember that you will probably have paid off your mortgage by the time you retire, and this should reduce your monthly bills substantially.**

Leaving it till later

If you haven't put much aside for your retirement – and that date is fast approaching – don't panic. There are steps that you can take. You will have to use a different plan because you won't have decades for your fund to grow. Try to put as much as you can into your pension fund every month, every year that you have left. For many people this can be the most suitable way of managing their money. In the early years of their working life they may have preferred to spend any spare cash they had on holidays, the children and their home. But if you fall into this group, it does mean that you will have to be paying the maximum that you can into your fund in later years. Bear in mind that:

- You may be able to make back payments if you haven't fully funded your pension for the past six years. See page 24 for full details
- Maybe you will be inheriting money or a family home that you could use to fund some of your retirement
- You may have savings plans that you started years ago and have forgotten about
- Old bank accounts are easy to trace now. Fill in a Dormant Bank Account form and hand it in to your local branch. From the details you supply the bank should be able to trace whether or not you still have an account at one of their branches. The forms should be available over the counter or from the British Bankers Association website. www.bba.org.uk.

Expert tip: If you can't even remember which bank your account was with, photocopy the form once you've filled it in and send a copy to all of the main banks.

Part-time work

When you give up your full-time job, you may be able to continue in the same business on a part-time basis or do something completely different just for a few hours a week. What you earn won't affect your entitlement to a pension but it may mean that you will be able to put off taking your pension for a few years. This means it will be worth more to you when it does click in.

But the money you earn will come into the tax equation. Many pensioners seem to believe in the myth that they won't have to pay tax when they retire. Sadly, they will if their earnings, including their pension and interest from any savings, are above the tax threshold.

Women and retirement planning

Women are different when it comes to pensions. They often retire earlier than men and live longer – which means they need a larger lump sum to buy the same amount of pension. And that can be more difficult to fund if they have taken a career break to bring up their family.

Women who are living with someone, but are not actually married, may not qualify for a widow's pension if anything happens to their partner.

On top of that, many women receive some of their husband's pension as part of a divorce settlement. This may not be enough to live on in retirement, and may be worth nothing at all if their ex-husband dies before he reaches retirement age. For more information on this see *Getting Divorced*, another title in this series.

It is crucially important for women to check on their own

pension arrangements and not just assume that their partner or husband is making enough provision.

Action plan

Don't take the ostrich approach, putting your head in the sand and hoping that the problem will go away. You don't need me to tell you that this is not going to sort itself out. There are certain steps you really must take. But don't take them alone. Read the action plan below and try to use it, with the help of all the details in the next chapter.

Here's what you have to do:

- Work out how much you currently have in any pension schemes you have.

To do this you should:

- Write to the pension provider(s) and ask for an up-to-date estimate of what your fund is worth, and what it will provide you with at retirement
- Ask your employer what your pension is likely to be on retirement
- Check up on any pensions you have left behind when you changed jobs
- Find out how much of a state pension you will receive
- Work out how much you will need on retirement
- Work out if your pension provision is on course to fund this
- Work out how you will fill any gap.

3 Pensions

- ⇨ **Your pension – what have you got and what will you need**
- ⇨ **Saving in a pension – the best option for you**
- ⇨ **Pensions v ISAs: the choice is yours**

Congratulations. You've taken the most difficult step of all. By reading this chapter you have taken that all-important decision to be in control of your pension – to sort it out properly.

You may have to write a few letters and do a few sums, but don't worry, it's not rocket science and you will be able to cope easily. Don't panic that at the end you will be forced to pay huge tracts of your income into your pension fund. You won't. But what you will have are the options.

You'll know:

- How much it suits you to pay into your pension
- The most effective way of using that money
- What you are likely to have in your retirement pot when you finally give up work.

And with that sort of information to hand, you'll be able to cope with the rest of your financial planning for retirement.

Quite simply, what you have to do is work your way through four main areas:

1 Work out how much you have saved in a pension already
2 Find out if there is too little in your pension pot
3 Understand the pension options for adding more cash

4   Decide if saving in a pension fund is better for you than
    using an ISA.

Need to know: **If you can join your company pension scheme
but havn't, sign up now! Otherwise you're probably turning
down a cash handout from your boss in the form of employer's contributions.**

How big is my pension pot?

Before you can work out whether you need to pay any extra
towards your pension, you need to know how much you
already have. And that means everything including your state
pension. So start collecting information.

State pension

1   Contact your local Benefits Agency – it's in the business
    pages of your telephone directory listed under
    Government Offices, in your local Yellow Pages, or you
    can ring 0191 218 7585 or log on to www.dss.gov.uk.
2   Ask for form BR19 which will give you a forecast of your
    state pension.
3   Fill it in and send it off to the Benefits Agency.

Company or occupational pension

• If you work for a large company or organisation and don't
  automatically get an annual statement, contact the
  pensions department and ask for an estimate of your
  likely pension on retirement.

- If your employer doesn't have a pensions department, look out your last pensions statement. That will show the name and address of the pensions provider. Write and ask for an estimate of your likely pension on retirement.

Personal pension plan (PPP)
- If you are funding your own pension – because you are self-employed or your employer doesn't run a pension scheme – write to the pension provider and ask how much your pension fund could be worth at retirement.

Pensions you used to pay into
- Contact the trustees of any occupational pension scheme you used to be a member of (or write to the company if you don't have contact details) to find out the value of your frozen pensions.

Need to know: **If you've lost track of your company pension, you can contact the Pension Schemes Registry, PO Box 1NN, Newcastle-upon-Tyne, NE99 1NN and ask for a tracing form, or get one on the internet at www.opra.gov.uk.**

Reading the replies

State pension You will be told whether you are on target for the full state pension, where the gaps are in your contributions if there are any, and what sort of earnings related top-up (SERPs) you might get.

Company/occupational pension Depending on the type of pension you have signed up for, information will be given to you in different ways.

Final salary schemes Your forecast should show the pension you are currently in line for. Although it is normally worked out as a percentage of your final salary, it should be expressed to you in pounds and pence. Obviously, you won't know your final salary, but depending on how far away from retirement you are, you should have a reasonable idea of the sort of pension you will receive. Any pensions you left behind when you moved jobs should be able to give you a more accurate picture of what you are likely to get.

Money purchase schemes You should be told the size of the pension fund you are likely to have.

Personal pension When you write and ask for an estimate of your likely pension you will need to give your policy number, and the date you might want to retire. You will receive back from the pension provider a letter with what is technically known as an 'illustration of projected funds'.

This will tell you the likely size of your pension fund on your retirement. It can be a little difficult to read at first glance but it's worth going through it carefully. The figures are not an accurate amount that you will get when you retire and they don't allow for inflation, so they will look bigger than they will be when you finally get the money. Much depends on how your fund grows over the years, but it will be the best guess of the pension provider and usually shows what your fund would be assuming three different growth rates.

Warning: **The figures you'll get look daunting. But it's vital that you have a realistic idea of what your pension will be. If you don't understand anything, ask.**

Is there a shortfall?

By now you have a rough idea of how much you are likely to get at retirement. The question is – will it be enough?

As a rough guide you need £100,000 in your pension pot at age 65 to give you an income of £10,000 year.

The chances are that your fund may be nowhere near that figure. Don't panic. Remember you may have money coming from other sources. The state pension, your home, other savings, maybe an inheritance – see Chapter 2 for full details.

But if you want to boost your pension income in retirement you will have to put more into your fund now. In order to choose the best option, it's important that you understand just what sort of pension you are currently funding.

Pension options

Like many things in life, pensions are not simple! Depending on whether you work for yourself or for a company that has a scheme, you could be paying into a:

- Final salary scheme
- Money purchase scheme
- Group personal pension plan
- Personal pension plan
- Stakeholder pension (from April 2001).

Final salary scheme

These are the traditional occupational pensions. Your pension will depend on two things:

- Your salary at retirement
- How long you've been a member of the pension scheme.

Normally, you and your employer will contribute to the scheme – though some schemes are funded solely by the employer. You will get your pension based on your final salary no matter how well or badly the fund performs.

Final salary pension schemes pay you a fraction of your salary, when you retire, for every year that you are a member of the scheme – usually $\frac{1}{80}$ or sometimes $\frac{1}{60}$. So if you have worked for the firm for 20 years you will receive $\frac{20}{60}$ ($\frac{1}{3}$) or $\frac{20}{80}$ ($\frac{1}{4}$) of your final salary. The maximum you are allowed by law to receive is $\frac{2}{3}$.

Final salary schemes:

- Give you certainty – your pension is guaranteed
- Depend on your salary at retirement.

Money purchase scheme

Here again, you and your employer contribute to a pension fund. When you retire the pension you get depends on how much has been paid in and how well the investments have done. There are no guarantees as to what you will receive.

Money purchase schemes:

- Are dependent on how well the fund has been invested
- Do not let you spend the whole pension fund directly; you have to buy an annuity.

Group personal pension plan

A group personal pension (GPP) is often set up within the firm that you work for. Your employer will almost certainly make a contribution, but it is not a company pension. It is *your* pension – the contract is between you and the pension provider. But it can be cheaper than having your own fund because the 'bulk buying' effect may reduce charges. What you get at retirement depends on how much has been paid into the fund, and how well the investments have done over the years.

Group personal pension plans:

- Will allow you to continue to pay money in after you have moved to another job
- Are generally better than personal pensions because your employer will probably contribute to them.

Personal pension plan

Anyone whose employer doesn't run a pension scheme, or who is self-employed, can take out a personal pension (although the rules change in April 2001 with the arrival of stakeholder pensions; see page 20). The amount you can pay into a personal pension varies according to your age (see table on next page).

You simply pay in contributions, either monthly or in a lump sum once a year, and your money is invested on your behalf. The pension company will make a charge for managing your money but you can choose the type of fund you want your money to be invested in.

In the past there has been a lot of criticism because the charges have been high and the schemes were often quite inflexible. Some plans penalised you heavily if you wanted to stop making contributions for a while, perhaps because you were taking a career break or your business was going through a downturn. Some even charged if you increased the amount you paid in. But the arrival of stakeholder, with its low charges, has changed all that. There are a number of personal pensions on offer with reasonable charges, flexibility and a consistent track record of performance. To find the best for you, check the tables in pension magazines or ask a specialist financial adviser.

Personal pensions:

- Are suitable for people without access to a company pension scheme, or who are self-employed
- Have limits on the amounts you can pay in, according to your age.

Personal pension limits

Age	Pension contribution as a % of earnings
35 or below	17.5
36–45	20
46–50	25
51–55	30
56–60	35
61 or over	40

Not all of your earnings will count – only what are known as net relevant earnings. If you are self-employed it usually means your profits before tax.

> *Warning:* You can only pay into one type of pension at a time. So don't try to mix and match company and personal schemes.

Stakeholder pension

This is a new type of pension, which you can contribute to from April 2001. It is designed to help people who in the past have been put off buying a pension because they think they can't afford it. Stakeholder will have lower costs than many personal pensions – limited to 1% a year – and will accept premiums as low as £20 a month.

From October 2001, companies with five or more employees will have to set up a stakeholder pension scheme for their employees. Employers don't have to contribute towards the fund – though many will – but they do have to make a scheme available to employees. Costs and charges will be low, but the choice of investment funds may also be fairly limited.

If you are self-employed you can choose a stakeholder pension to take advantage of the low costs and charges. But check out the scheme you currently have running. Many providers have reduced charges on current schemes to bring them into line with stakeholder.

If you are thinking of moving from one scheme to another, take advice from a pensions professional first.

Boosting your pension

Having worked out what you are likely to get from your pension at retirement, you will probably want to give your

fund a boost. How you do it depends on what sort of pension
you have. Here are the options:
- State pension
- Company pension
- Personal pension
- Stakeholder pension.

State pension

If your BR 19 shows that you won't be entitled to the full
state pension, you may be able to put more money in.
Anyone entitled to make full National Insurance contributions over the previous six years, but who has some gaps,
can go back and make up those payments. However, if you
were paying the married woman's NI rate, you cannot. The
form will tell you where your NI gaps are. Try to make the
payments if you can.

> *Need to know:* **The government is planning to introduce a
> combined pension forecast including state, company and per-
> sonal pensions. Everyone will be sent an annual statement
> telling them how much of a pension they are likely to receive
> in retirement.**

Company pension

If you're a member of a company pension scheme, there are
several routes you can take to top up your pension. You could
put money into:
- Added years
- AVC (additional voluntary contribution)

- Free-standing AVC
- Stakeholder (from April 2001).

Don't be put off by the jargon, it's not as difficult to understand as it seems.

Added years
This applies to employees in final salary schemes. It simply means you are buying extra years of pension membership. The cost of the added years will depend on your age when you start buying them and is worked out as a percentage of your earnings. Check the rules of your scheme.

Added years:
- Are worthwhile if your salary is likely to carry on rising sharply
- Are worth considering for anyone who is financially cautious because you will not be dependent on investment performance.

AVC
Additional voluntary contributions allow you to make extra payments into a fund that is run by the main pension scheme. Your employer may pay some of the charges and costs, which means that more of your money is put away to grow for your retirement. But your choice of fund will be restricted – some pension schemes offer only one low-risk fund (usually with-profits) and possibly a deposit account.

AVCs:
- Usually have low costs and charges
- Have a limited choice of funds.

Free-standing AVC
With a free-standing AVC (FSACV), you buy your pension top-up directly from a pension provider, rather than going through your pension scheme. You can choose from any of the hundreds of private pension funds that are available. But it is almost always a much more expensive option than choosing the in-house route.

Free-standing AVCs:
- Give you a wide choice of funds to invest in
- Are more expensive than in-house AVCs.

Cash caution: **The maximum you can pay into your occupational pension and AVC combined is 15% of your total earnings. So if you are paying 5% into your main pension scheme, you can pay an extra 10% into an AVC.**

Stakeholder pension
From April 2001, anyone earning less than £30,000 a year can use a stakeholder as a top-up plan – and pay in a maximum of £3,600 a year – and still keep their occupational pension. This means if you earn less than £30,000 a year, then a stakeholder could be a cheaper option than AVCs.

Stakeholders also let you take 25% of your pension fund tax-free at retirement, which AVCs do not – and this could be a big advantage. Your company schemes don't have to offer the stakeholder top-up option; it will be up to each one to decide.

You can also contribute up to £3,600 a year whether you are working or not – so you can carry on paying into one even if you leave your job.

Stakeholders:
- Are more flexible than AVCs
- Let you take 25% of your cash tax-free.

Personal pensions

Your personal pension is your own fund to do what you like with. You can pay more into the scheme you already have up and running, or start another one. If you have a regular premium plan you may want to put lump sum payments into a different scheme. There is no limit to the number of PPPs you can open in any tax year as long as the total you are paying in doesn't breach the Inland Revenue thresholds. (See table on page 19.)

Cash saver: It is usually cheaper to put a lump sum into a pension scheme, rather than increase your monthly payments. Ask your financial adviser or pension company which option is the most cost-effective.

Carry-back carry-forward

Ignore the clumsy term; this is a really useful way of getting extra tax relief by paying in extra to top up your personal pension plan. What the concessions give you is the ability to fund any pensions shortfall you may have had over the past six years.

But don't delay – the government is changing the rules from 5th April 2001 as part of its plans to bring in a new stakeholder pension. So you will have to move fast if you want to make full use of the scheme.

Personal pensions:
- Are a flexible way of building up a pension pot
- Allow you to pay in more as you get older.

Pensions v ISAs

Just because you are trying to put money aside for your retirement does not mean you have to use a pension. There are
other options (see Chapter 4). But individual savings accounts (ISAs) are a particularly suitable alternative for many
of us, because they are more flexible than a pension.

The main advantage of an ISA is that you have much more
freedom about when you take your money – and how you
take it. You have to use part of your pension pot to buy a
pension (annuity) and that pension dies with you, or your
spouse, so there is a lot to be said for having a split of pension
and investments. Then your money can be left to your depen-
dants when you die.

You can cash in your ISA any time, and for any reason, and
you don't have to buy an annuity with the money. This means
you won't be tied into annuity rates and rules – unlike with a
personal pension. Your cash isn't locked away until you retire
and it all comes out of the fund tax-free.

The downside is that you have paid tax on the money (up
to £7,000 a year) going into an ISA, whereas anything you pay
into your pension goes in with a tax handout from the government in the form of tax relief.

But don't think that you have to choose between a pension
and an ISA. You can have both – providing you have the funds.

> *Cash caution:* Watch out if you are the type of person who finds it hard to be disciplined about saving. Putting your money into an ISA, where you will be able to spend it before retirement, may mean you do just that.

So what are the pros and cons, and how do you decide which is best for you?

Personal pensions

Pros
- Give you tax relief on contributions up to your highest rate.
- Have higher limits for contributions – especially as you get older.
- Will let you take up to 25% of your pension fund as a tax-free cash lump sum.
- There is no inheritance tax to pay on the pension fund if you die.
- Grow free of income and capital gains tax.

Cons
- Can have high costs and charges.
- Are less flexible when you come to take out your money.
- Will not let you access your fund until your chosen retirement date without penalties.

ISAs

Pros
- Proceeds are tax-free when you cash in your fund.
- Money grows free of income tax and capital gains tax.
- Can be accessed quite easily.

Cons
- Strict limits on how much you can pay in a year.
- No tax relief on contributions.
- Could tempt you to spend the money early.
- Your ISA could be subject to inheritance tax if you die.

> *Expert tip:* If you are a higher-rate taxpayer, you will probably find that the tax advantages of a pension outweigh the disadvantages.

Checklist
- What sort of pension do I have?
- Do I know how much it will be worth when I retire?
- Will I be entitled to the full state pension?
- What is the best option for me to top up my pension?
- Would I be better off with an ISA?

4 Investments

⇨ **Are you a risk taker – work it out**
⇨ **Your savings – the pick of the plans**
⇨ **Your investments – check out the choices**

By the time you reach your 40s, and more particularly your 50s, you should be finding you can ease your financial belt a notch or two.

So what do you do with the extra cash? The temptation might be to spend it – on a bigger car or more expensive holidays perhaps. Somehow, we always seem to live up to our income.

But think ahead to the time when you will no longer have a regular wage coming in. Putting aside some of that spare cash can reap dividends in the future. Moderating your holiday plans now might mean that you have a more comfortable retirement.

Check first that your pension is under control. If it's not, turn back to Chapter 3 for more information.

Then think about whether you want to put your spare cash into a savings account or invest it in shares. You'll need to work out your attitude to risk.

Understanding risk

There are two main ways of locking up your money for the future:

- Saving it
- Investing it.

Saving – putting your cash into a bank or building society account where interest will be added

Investing – putting your money into shares, bonds or property where the growth will mainly come from the increase in value of what you bought.

On the face of it, investing for capital growth seems riskier because the value of the shares, bonds or property that you have bought can fall. But some experts think that using a savings account for your retirement cash is riskier because you never get the chance for capital growth on your money, and even low levels of inflation will eat away at the real value of your nest egg.

If you know it would worry you to see any shares that you buy falling in value, then investing in the stockmarket is not for you.

Work out now whether you want to:

- Keep all your money in a savings account
- Invest in shares, bonds or property in the hope of capital growth
- Spread your risk by saving and investing.

Building up savings

First things first. You will need some rainy day money to cover any financial emergency that might arise. How much is 'enough' will depend on your own circumstances. For some it may be a few hundred pounds; others may need enough to carry them through several months without work.

> *Cash caution:* Only lock your money away in 30-day or 60-day notice accounts if you might be tempted to dip in and spend it. You don't get much more in interest, and it can cost you dear if you need the cash in a hurry.

Look at the interest rates currently on offer and open an account with a top payer.

Check the rate you are getting on any current savings. If you can do at least 1% better elsewhere, switch.

Longer-term savings will be better off in an ISA – an individual savings account. The money will grow tax-free which makes the rate of interest seem higher.

You can invest up to £3,000 in cash in a tax year. You can also invest in shares through an ISA, but the rules are complicated and if you break them the Inland Revenue will close down some of your accounts.

In total you can put £7,000 into an ISA in a tax year. The rules about how you invest the money are very specific and quite complicated.

> *Warning:* If you intend having cash and shares in an ISA, be very careful how you buy. Take advice from someone who understands the system.

Investing for your future

If you can leave your money invested for five years or more and you are prepared to take some risk, then you should be looking at shares. Research shows that, over the longer term, your money will be worth more invested in the stockmarket than in a savings account.

But there are degrees of risk within the stockmarket. The more specialised your investment, the higher the risk but the greater can be your chances of doing really well.

> *Warning:* **If you put all your money into one share, in a high-risk sector such as medical research or the internet, you may find your money trebles, but it could be that the company goes under and you lose everything.**

So, it's time again to think about how much risk you want to take.

One low-risk option is to invest in a fund. You can choose unit trusts, open ended investment companies (OEICs) and investment trusts. Ignore the rather dry terms and just think of them as a practical and affordable way of letting you buy a wide variety of shares.

For as little as £25 a month you can buy into one of these types of funds and your money will be invested in hundreds of different companies. Some funds with the lowest risk will keep some of their money in cash or commercial property to spread the risk still further.

> *Home truth:* Investment trusts are usually cheaper than unit trusts, and figures show that over the longer term they usually perform better. But you have to be comfortable with the higher level of risk.

Actively managed funds

You can choose a fund that is managed by a professional fund manager who decides which shares to buy and sell and when to do it. There will be a charge for this.

Tracker funds

These funds are operated by a computer programme which buys the shares that make up a particular stockmarket index (such as the Footsie 100 – the 100 largest companies in Britain, or the Footsie 250, which includes 250 of the biggest names) and as the index rises and falls, so does the tracker fund. The charges are usually quite a bit lower because you are not paying for a team of managers.

> *Cash caution:* Tracker funds may be cheaper than managed ones, but they are not lower risk.

OEICs are relatively new players in the field. They are supposed to be gradually replacing unit trusts, but so far the process has been very slow. Only a limited number of investment companies offer OEICs. The main advantage they have over unit trusts is that their charges are easier to understand.

Which is suitable for me?
- Unit trusts are a fairly low-risk pooled stockmarket investment. You can vary the levels of risk you take. Investing in a managed fund will reduce your risk level; selecting one particular sector – such as small companies or East Asia or high-tech funds – will increase it.
- OEICs have a similar risk level to unit trusts, but have simpler charges. However, not many companies currently offer OEICs.
- Investment trusts are riskier because they are made up of shares, but they are cheaper to buy and can perform better in the long term.

Choosing a fund

Whatever type of fund you go for, it's important to buy into one that is likely to grow in value.
- Check past performance figures to help you decide where to invest your money
- Avoid the catchy headlines in newspaper adverts and instead buy a personal finance magazine or check the weekend papers for best buy tables
- Don't simply look at the performance over the last five or 10 years, but find out how the fund did over each year. It could be that one spectacular year made up for three or four miserable ones.

Need to know: Before you invest in a fund that has been performing well, check that the fund manager is still there. Star fund managers are often poached by other firms and the fund could now be in less experienced hands.

Shares

You can invest directly in shares, and plenty of small investors do nowadays. The risk of losing money is greater than if you are in a fund, but so is the chance of making your nest egg grow. You can get plenty of information on companies and sectors from the internet, in newspapers, and from specialist magazines. Read before you buy your shares or log on to some websites: www.FTyourmoney.com, www.uk-invest.co.uk or www.fool.co.uk.

Try to spread your risk by having a portfolio with a clutch of shares in different sectors. And keep an eye on what you buy.

There are costs to buying shares but you can keep these as low as possible by dealing through internet or telephone based brokers.

Some would-be investors who don't feel up to going it alone in shares form an Investment Club with a group of friends. They all pay a certain amount every month – usually around £25 each – and then decide together which shares to buy. It can be great fun, not least because the monthly meetings are often in a local pub. Of course you can still lose money, but it does spread your risk into more shares than your own money could buy, and it gives you a chance to hear why others like, or want to avoid, a particular company or sector.

More details from ProShare on 020 7220 1755 or www.proshare.org.

ISAs

Try to invest in shares through an ISA if you can.

You have an allowance of £7,000 for tax year 2000/01 – and you can put the whole lot in shares if you wish or you can split your money between shares, cash and insurance.

> *Watch out:* ISAs come in two types – minis and maxis. A maxi ISA means you can invest the full amount with one ISA provider – either split into shares and cash etc or just shares. A mini ISA gives you the freedom to get each part from a different provider, but you cannot take out a mini and a maxi ISA in the same tax year.

Checklist

- How much risk am I prepared to take?
- Do I want savings, investments or a mixture of the two?
- Do I understand how funds work?
- Do I want to invest directly in shares, or is that too risky for me?
- Should I be investing in an ISA?

5 Your health

⇨ **Private health care – how to afford it**
⇨ **If illness strikes, could you cope financially**
⇨ **Should you plan ahead for long-term care**

One of the large expenses you might have to write into your retirement planning is looking after your health. Many of us may have been lucky enough to have made it into our 40s or 50s without too much going medically wrong. A quick trip to the GP will usually sort things out. But as we look ahead to older age it makes financial sense to have some provision for ill health. Paying to go privately can be costly. Hospital stays, serious perhaps even chronic illnesses and residential or nursing homes are all frighteningly expensive. As we get older, we may feel less comfortable relying on the hard-pressed NHS.

Department of Health figures show that at times recently there have been over a million people waiting for treatment that a consultant has advised them they need. As hospitals fail to cope with demand, particularly in the winter, patients are dying because essential operations have to be cancelled.

So what sort of cover might you think of buying? There are three main areas to consider.
- Private medical insurance
- Critical illness
- Long-term care.

Private medical insurance

This sort of cover is designed to pay your medical bills and treatment, as and when you need it. At the top end it will cover all your consultant's bills, outpatients' costs, operations, your stay in hospital, any home nursing you need and all of your drugs and dressings. The problem is that it is very expensive and the price goes up as you get older and are more likely to make a claim. Soaring premiums have pushed the full cost out of the reach of many people, so the providers have come up with various schemes designed to bring down the cost. But this does also cut the cover.

It may suit you to buy a cheaper, budget plan, but do make sure you know exactly what you are getting for your money. Here are some of the ways you can crop your premiums.

- Offer to pay the first part of every claim – excesses range from £100 right up to £5,000
- Accept a restricted hospital or consultant list
- Choose a policy that excludes certain medical procedures
- Agree to be treated on the NHS if the waiting list is short
- Offer to pay for outpatient consultations.

Cash caution: **Buying medical insurance can be very complicated because of the number of policies on the market, all offering different options. Take advice from a specialist broker. The Association of Medical Insurance Intermediaries will be able to give you a list, tel 0800 421 216.**

Once you decide to take out a policy you may have to fill in a form detailing any relevant medical history. Previous illnesses may not be covered by your policy if they recur. Don't be tempted to be economical with the truth here. If you have to make a claim, the insurance company will invariably check your medical records.

Cash saver: **Some insurance companies offer no-claim or low-claim discounts. It may be worth your while not to make a claim for small bills.**

Self-pay

You may not want to pay hundreds, if not thousands, of pounds each year for medical insurance. Some people save the premiums themselves and pay for any treatment or operations as and when they need them.

What you pay depends on where you go. It is definitely worth phoning around to find out about costs before you commit yourself.

Typical costs

Hip replacement	£5,500–10,000
Cataract	£1,275–2,560
Varicose vein removal	£1,050–1,850
Hernia	£1,050–2,025

Source: Health Care Navigator

If you can't afford to pay for the operation in advance some of the providers offer interest-free loans – but you must pay off the loan within 12 months otherwise you will be charged interest. Or you could set up a fixed rate loan in advance.

Need to know: You can pay your bills after the operation, or buy a packaged plan in advance from some hospitals. The package will be more expensive but if any complications arise, you won't have additional costs.

Critical illness

These are policies which pay out a lump sum if you are diagnosed as having a serious, life-threatening illness such as cancer, a stroke, multiple sclerosis or a heart attack. The list of illnesses is pre-set so you will know, before you buy your policy, exactly what is covered.

Expert tip: Don't opt for the policy that offers the most illnesses just because it seems as if you are getting more for your money. Over 90% of claims are for cancer or heart attack.

If you are diagnosed as having one of the illnesses on the list, the lump sum will be paid to you and can be used for anything you choose: paying off your mortgage, converting your house to make your life easier, buying medical equipment that you need or just taking a holiday.

The policy can run for:

- The rest of your life – whole of life insurance
- A set number of years – term insurance.

Whole of life You pay the premiums for the rest of your life, or until you start to claim. This sort of policy may suit those who feel they would never be able to cope financially if a serious illness was to hit them.

Term insurance You only pay the premiums and get the cover for a set number of years. This may suit those who want the lump sum to cover something specific, such as their mortgage, or the children getting through university. It may be an option if you don't want to continue paying the premiums when you retire or you think you'll be financially comfortable once you have the lump sum from your pension.

You choose in advance the size of the lump sum you would want paid out, and the premiums are set accordingly. The larger the lump sum, the higher the premiums will be.

To cover a lump sum of £20,000 that would be paid out whenever the illness was diagnosed, the following monthly payments are typical:

- A non-smoking man of 40...£25
- A non-smoking woman of 40...£21

If the cover was only for 25 years, so that it stopped at age 65, the same two people would pay:

- 40 year-old man..£15
- 40 year-old woman...£13

Once you reach 50 the premiums will rise:

- 50 year-old non-smoking man for whole of life policy ...£43
- 50 year-old non-smoking woman £35

For 15 year cover to run to age 65:

- 50 year-old man..£23
- 50 year-old woman...£19

> ***Cash caution:*** **Many providers charge a minimum premium of £20–25 a month. If you are affected by this, increase the lump sum to the level that £25 would fund.**

Remember that these premiums may not be fixed. They are often reviewed, and probably increased, at least every five years, sometimes more frequently.

Long-term care

In your 40s or 50s it is difficult to think so far down the road that you want to plan for your very old age. Long-term care is expensive and most of us choose not to think about it until we have to. Not everyone will need care in their old age. It's estimated that one in five of those aged over 80 will need care at some point. That means that four out of five won't.

However, if you do need it, you'll find that it is not cheap. On average, nursing home care costs around £25,000 a year, and a residential home costs around £13,000. Anyone with Alzheimer's disease or senile dementia, requiring intensive nursing care, can expect to pay £35,000–40,000 a year.

But you may not have to fund a lump sum of anything like that size. Remember that if an illness like this hits you once you retire you will have an income from your pension that can be diverted to nursing home fees, or you could sell your home and use some of the funds from that. If you can continue to live at home, because your partner or someone else is able to care for you, you may be entitled to Attendance allowance. It is not means tested, but how much you get depends on how much care you need.

Need to know: **If you have less than £10,000 in capital, the state will pay the full costs of your long-term care. If you have more than £16,000 then you have to foot the bill. Between these two figures, there's a sliding scale where you split the bill. The value of your home won't be taken into account if your spouse or partner lives there.**

Paying for long-term care

The advantage of a long-term care policy is that the policy pays your expenses for life, once you make your claim. You don't have to worry about growing bills and you shouldn't need to move to a cheaper nursing home because your cash has run out. If you want to take out private insurance to pay for long-term care, you have two choices:

- Monthly premiums
- A lump sum payment.

Monthly premiums The earlier you start, the cheaper is the insurance. But you could find that you're paying into a policy for may years before you need it. And you may not need it at all. The premiums will rise as you get older, and you could find it hard to afford to pay, just when you might need the policy most.

Lump sum payment Alternatively, you can buy a long-term care policy using a lump sum. This may make the policy affordable if you have a nest egg from trading down your house, or perhaps from your pension. But remember that once you pay over the money it is gone for good.

Claiming
Once you take out a regular premium long-term care policy, you pay the premiums for the rest of your life, or until you need to claim. Usually your claim will be accepted when you can no longer perform at least three of the so-called Activities of Daily Living, such as dressing and feeding yourself, and going to the toilet.

How to choose
Very few of us could afford to fund all these types of policies. And which you go for will be an individual decision. But it is worth drawing up a list of pros and cons for each and then discussing the issue with your partner and perhaps the rest of your family too. You may also need to take some advice from a specialist in this area.

6 Tax

⇨ **Use the tax breaks to cut your bills**
⇨ **Build your own tax haven**

If there's one thing we all grudge paying … it's tax. So don't pay more than you have to.

Don't cheat to pay less – that's *evasion* and it's illegal.

Use the system to pay less – that's *avoidance* and it makes good financial sense.

There are lots of tax breaks available, some easier to understand than others. If you have a lot of money you may need an accountant or tax expert to help you through the maze. For the rest of us there are several well-trodden paths that are worth following.

Check out:
• Your savings
• ISAs
• PEPs and TESSAs
• Your pension
• Offshore accounts.

Your savings

It may be worth moving your money around. Any savings you have in bank or building society accounts will be taxed as though you are an ordinary-rate tax payer. That means the interest will have the tax taken off before you get it.

Non-taxpayers
If you don't earn enough to pay tax, sign form R85 in your branch to have the interest paid gross

10% payers
If you pay tax at the lowest rate, you don't have to fill in a complicated self-assessment tax form to claim back the money you are due. Use the much simpler R40 form which you can get from your local tax office or the Inland Revenue Enquiry Office, or ask for a copy of the explanatory leaflet IR110, *A Guide for People with Savings*, which you can also get from the Revenue's website. www.inlandrevenue.gov.uk.

High-rate taxpayers
If you are a high-rate taxpayer, think about moving some of your money to accounts that pay interest tax-free such as National Savings Certificates. But remember, the interest rate is really only worthwhile if you hold the certificates for the full term. A two-year fixed interest saving certificate paying 4.5% tax-free is worth:
- 5.6% to an ordinary-rate taxpayer
- 7.5% to a high-rate taxpayer.

Expert tip: **If your partner is taxed at a lower rate than you, it may be an idea to move your savings into their name. That way you will pay less tax on the interest the money earns.**

ISAs

Individual savings accounts are a great way to shine up your savings and investments. All the money you put in – and you can pay in up to £7,000 a tax year – grows tax-free. You can invest the whole amount in shares, or split the money between shares, savings and life insurance – for full details see Chapter 4. If you are investing in shares – either directly in companies or through unit or investment trusts or OEICs – make sure you buy them in an ISA, if you can, so that you don't have to pay capital gains tax (CGT). That may not be a worry now but as your portfolio grows you could find yourself liable for CGT in the future. Take steps now to avoid that – invest through an ISA.

Need to know: **There are strict rules about what sorts of ISAs you can buy and how much you can invest each year. Make sure you understand them before you sign up.**

Anyone wanting to put some rainy day money into a savings account should do it through an ISA too. The interest will grow tax-free, even if you are a taxpayer. But you have to be careful about the sort of ISA you open – if you want to mix shares and savings take advice before you sign up to anything.

Expert tip: **You don't lose the tax relief if you withdraw your money, so you could use an ISA savings account even for short-term money. But remember, once you have taken the cash out, you can't put it back in again.**

PEPs and TESSAs

You can't put any new money into PEPs or set up a new TESSA. But keep an eye on any that you already have.

PEPs Make sure that the fund is still giving you good returns. You'll get statements every year or six months telling you how your money is growing. If it's not doing well, consider switching to another fund management company. The transfer will probably cost you money, and there are no guarantees that the new company will give you better performance, so take advice before you make the move.

Expert tip: **Make sure that you switch from one PEP to another PEP. Don't take your money out of the first and then assume you can open another – you won't be able to do that and the tax break will be lost forever.**

TESSAs Millions of savers still have TESSAs up and running and sheltering cash from the tax man. Some have already saved the full £9,000 but many have set aside much less than that. If your TESSA has less than the maximum in it, don't forget to top it up every year so that you have as much as you can earning interest tax-free. Once your TESSA matures move the capital into a special TESSA/ISA account. You can't move the interest. Under the rules, that has to be invested elsewhere – or you could spend it. And keep a check on interest rates. Some accounts are paying very low rates.

Tessa limits
Year 1   up to £3,000
Years 2–5 up to £1,800 a year
(In year 5 up to £600 if you have previously paid in the maximum)

Your pension

Any money that you put into your pension goes in 'gross', which means you don't pay tax on it.

Every £100 that goes into your pension fund:
- Costs an ordinary-rate taxpayer £78
- Costs a high-rate taxpayer £60.

The Inland Revenue contributes the rest, so from the tax point of view, pensions are a bargain. See Chapter 2 to work out how much you will need.

Offshore accounts

You may be tempted by higher interest rates to put your money in an offshore account. This does not mean that you don't have to pay any tax on the interest, or that you can go on holiday and just spend your way through your funds. If your account earns interest you have to pay tax on the money. But there are still advantages – though they are more subtle than you might expect.
- Interest is paid gross. You do still have to pay the tax but usually not for a year after the interest is paid
- Interest rates can be higher than at your local branch.

Having money in an offshore account does NOT mean that you can hide the funds from the Inland Revenue or not declare the interest on your self-assessment form. That would be illegal.

However, if you work abroad and are not paying UK tax, there can be huge advantages to moving your savings offshore. Take advice from a tax expert before moving your funds.

If you decide to open an offshore account, choose a branch of a UK bank or building society and your money should be as safe as it would be if it remained on the mainland.

Helpful web addresses

There's a lot of useful tax information available on the charity TaxAid's website – www.TaxAid.co.uk – or try the Inland Revenue itself www.inlandrevenue.gov.uk.

Checklist

- Am I getting the best tax deal on my savings?
- Have I checked whether an ISA is suitable for me?
- Have I looked at my PEPs and TESSAs recently?
- Is my pension underfunded?
- Should I have some of my savings offshore?

7 Inheritance

⇨ **Make a will, it won't kill you**
⇨ **Enduring Power of Attorney – why you need one**

There's one financial fact that's a certainty – however much money you have in this life you can't take it with you to the next. But you can make sure that what you leave behind goes exactly where you want it to. And usually that's not the pockets of the Inland Revenue.

So:

*   Make sure you have an up-to-date will
*   Do some basic inheritance tax planning.

Your will

Thousands of people put off making a will because they feel it might be a jinx. Well, let's explode that myth right away. We are all going to die, and making a will won't bring that day any closer, or push it further away. So get started right now. It's unfair to put the burden of sorting out your affairs on those you leave behind, particularly at a time when they will be emotionally stressed by your death.

On top of that, your money may not go to the people you assume will benefit. There are very strict rules about who gets what if you die without having written a will (that's known as dying intestate). An unmarried partner, for instance, may receive nothing no matter how long you had been together. The term 'common law wife' or 'common law husband' has no legal standing.

Warning: **The rules on what happens to your money when you die don't take account of modern day relationships. Your partner will probably receive nothing if you are not married so it's even more important for co-habiting couples to have wills.**

If you already have a will, re-read it. Any change in your circumstances, such as marriage or divorce, could mean your will is invalid or out of date. Some of the people mentioned in your will may have changed address or died, so check the details.

You can write your will yourself, use a legal website or buy a will pack from a stationers. But, unless your affairs are simple, this may prove to be a false economy. It can cost a lot of money to sort out a financial tangle after you die. Because it is a legal document, you may feel it's worth the expense of going to a lawyer.

Expert tip: **Check out charges before appointing a lawyer or banker as an executor. The fees can be very high – even on quite simple estates. It may be cheaper for your executor to pay for any professional help as and when they need it.**

Will costs

Using a lawyer – around £75–100 for a simple will. What you pay depends on how complicated your will is for the lawyer to draw up. But if your affairs are complicated, or you make a number of changes each time you see a draft, then the bill will rise.

Using the internet – around £20 if you download a standard will from an internet site. Your will should be checked by a lawyer but this is only suitable for people with simple affairs.

Buying a will pack – around £5. You get helpful notes with the pack, but your finished will won't be checked by a legal professional. If you do want it checked, that's likely to cost another £30 or so.

Documents

Make sure you keep your documents in a safe place where someone will be able to find them should anything happen to you. There are billions of pounds currently locked in dormant bank accounts, many in the names of people who have died without leaving the details, so make sure none of your money joins that pile.

Make a list of what you have, include relevant account numbers and the name and phone number of your stockbroker, financial adviser, bank, mortgage lender and so on.

Warning: **Make sure that your executors know where your will is, and the name and address of your solicitor, and that they have access to your list of important documents. You won't be able to come back and give them any details they can't find.**

Power of attorney

Many people who are in good health now worry about what will happen if their mental faculties deteriorate and they are no longer able to run their financial affairs. The answer is to have an Enduring Power of Attorney. This is a formal, legal document, drawn up by a lawyer, in which you appoint a person to take over the management of your financial affairs should you become mentally or physically unable to cope. You have to sign it, as does the person you appoint.

If the time comes for it to be implemented, the lawyer has to give notice to various relatives and then register the Enduring Power of Attorney with the Court of Protection. Without this document, your family would have to apply to the Court of Protection to appoint a Receiver to act for you – a slower and more costly process. And the person you would like to control your financial affairs may not be the one appointed.

An Enduring Power of Attorney costs around £100.

Inheritance tax planning

You don't have to be very rich nowadays to have to think about inheritance tax planning. With the dramatic rise in house prices over the past 25 years many more people could be caught in this trap. The critical figure is £234,000 (2000/01). If everything you own comes to more than that, you'll have to make some tax moves or your heirs will have to pay up.

There is no inheritance tax to pay on what you leave to your spouse – and it really does mean your married partner. But anything over £234,000 that you leave to anyone else – including long-term partners – will be taxed at a whopping 40%.

As people get much older, and often after their partner has died, they start to make specific moves to reduce any likely inheritance tax bill. You can give money away while you are alive, and, for example, on the wedding of a child. But for most people, it may be enough to ensure that your will is written in such a way that some of your assets are passed down to your children on your death rather than leaving everything to your spouse. That way, there can be some savings on any tax that might be paid.

Expert tip: **If you think you own enough to tip you into the inheritance tax bracket, take professional advice on the steps you should be taking. There are plenty of moves you can make, but they will affect your future finances.**

Inheriting from your parents

Many families now receive a huge financial boost in their middle years by inheriting a property or some money from their parents or other relatives. Often, people in their 40s or 50s are finding themselves with quite substantial sums of money. Tread carefully if you find that the total estate – not just the part of it that you are inheriting – amounts to more than the £234,000 inheritance tax level.

There are some moves you can make, even after someone has died, to mitigate any tax you might have to pay. You will need to take professional advice.

Once the money has come to you from an inheritance, there will be no further tax to be paid.

You may want to use the money to buy something as a keepsake or remembrance. Or you might add it in to your general financial planning. Work out where the greatest bene-fits would come to you.

Should you:

- Pay off part of the mortgage – reduce your monthly outgoings
- Top up your pension – increase your pension payments in retirement
- Add to your savings – cushion your emergency funds; increase your income from the interest
- Pay off any short-term loans you have – reduce your monthly outgoings for a few months or years
- Invest in shares – grow your lump sum for retirement.

Don't rush to spend or invest the money. At a time when you may still be emotionally upset by a death, it's wise to take your time before committing to a course of financial action. There will be little harm done by leaving the money in a savings account for a few months.

Checklist

- Is my will up-to-date?
- Do I need to make a (new) will?
- Should I draw up an Enduring Power of Attorney?
- Do I need to do any inheritance tax planning?

8 Stop all the alarm clocks

⇨ **The options as you approach retirement**
⇨ **Put your financial house in order**

The time will come, perhaps in the near future, when you have an actual date for stopping work. You probably can't wait. It's important to be financially prepared. And there's more to it than drinking your own health at the farewell party and resetting the alarm clock.

No work means no pay cheque at the end of every month. So before you give up, spend a little time thinking about the money you have and how you will cope in the months ahead.

If you are working for a large organisation, or a switched-on boss, you may be encouraged to go on a pre-retirement course. It will either be run internally, or you'll join others at a specially organised seminar. These courses should give you some pointers about what to expect from your pension, your finances and your health. Listen to what they say about your money, but don't sign up to any new plans until you have thought it all through.

You can't make your investment plans without knowing what you need in the first place. So try to work out – generally – what you think you will be spending. And don't forget to add in extras, like holidays. That should give you an idea of what sort of income you need. Now it's time to think about your finances.

- Your savings
- Your investments
- Your mortgage
- Your pension
- Your loans
- Your tax.

It may be that you won't have to make many changes at all, but it's worth spending an evening making sure that your finances are ready to put their feet up too.

Your savings

You may have some money in an account that you use for dipping in and out of, or for financial emergencies. It may be that you will be able to run this with a lower balance and tuck some cash away into an account paying higher levels of interest. Or you might want more money in this account, as there will be no salary coming in every month.

Things to do:
- Check the interest rates you are getting on your savings accounts. Some banks and building societies have an unnerving habit of reducing rates without you realising it. A quick phone call should sort that out. If you are not within 1% of top rates elsewhere, move your money. Remember to check for penalties first.
- Work out if you could put some of your money into a tax-free ISA. See Chapter 4 for more details.

> *Need to know:* **Make a diary note of the date when interest payments are made so that you can add that extra money into your budget.**

Things to think about:

- Have you got the right percentage of your money in savings? As you approach retirement you may feel more comfortable with less in risky investments and more in safe savings
- Should you switch your money from branch-based accounts to telephone or internet accounts to get higher rates of interest?
- Do you need to keep open accounts that are near to where you work? You may not be passing that way much in the future.

Your investments

Take a close look at how your money is invested. It may be that over the years you have opened various PEPs and ISAs, or bought unit and investment trusts. While you were working, you would have been looking for capital growth – that means you'd be hoping that the *value* of your funds would increase. Now, with less money coming in every month, you may want or need *income* from these investments as well. That probably means switching into different types of funds. You can do this with the same company, or go to a new one. But if your financial affairs are complicated, take some professional advice before you make any moves.

> *Cash caution:* **Always ask what the penalties are before you move your money from one fund to another. You may be able to cut some of the costs by, for instance, moving within the same company rather than switching to another. But if you don't know where the charges are, you won't be able to avoid them.**

Things to do:

- Make a list of any investments you've got and check that they are performing as well as you expected. Weekend papers and financial websites have this sort of information – usually set out as 'best buy' tables. If your investments are not up there with the winners, consider switching to a different company
- Check your risk profile. You may not feel comfortable taking as much risk with your investments once you retire
- Look at any shares you've got. Do you want to take the profits and move the money into more general, and less risky, funds?

Things to think about:

- Will you need income from your investments once you retire? If you do you may have to move some of your money from one type of fund to another. Take some professional advice before you make the switch
- Do you need to cash in some of your investments and move the money into risk-free savings accounts?

Your mortgage

Many homeowners, as they approach retirement, feel that they would like to have the mortgage paid off. If you have a repayment mortgage, you may be able to do this. Perhaps you have some savings, or are likely to take a lump sum from your pension. But if you have any sort of endowment mortgage – resist the temptation to cash it in. It is only in the last few years that the policy should really come into its own, with the real gains being made then. You could always use some of your savings to pay off part of the mortgage and so reduce your monthly payments.

If you will have difficulty making the repayments from your pension, go and see your mortgage provider or a financial adviser for some professional advice.

Things to do:
- Work out whether or not you will want to pay off your mortgage
- Work out how to afford it.

Things to think about:
- How will you fund your mortgage payments after you retire if you need to?

For full advice on what to do about the mortgage, see Chapter 9.

Your pension

It is crucial, as your approach retirement, that you know exactly where you stand with all your pensions. Your company pension should come to you automatically but others might not. If you are taking your pension early you should write and tell the provider just when you want the payments to start.

You will also have to make decisions about how much of your pension you want to take as a lump sum, what sort of provision you'll be making for your partner, and when you want the payments to start. See Chapter 10 for full details.

The state pension should come to you automatically in the week of your 60th or 65th birthday – though the rules for women are changing. Any woman who was younger than 45 when she saw in the millennium won't qualify for her state pension until she is 65.

Cash saver: **If you don't need the state pension immediately – perhaps because you are working on, or working part-time – you don't have to take it. The longer you put off, the more you'll get when you decide to take it.**

Things to do:
- Check that all the pension providers have your full and correct details
- Work out when you want the pension payments to start.

Things to think about:
- What are you going to do with the lump sum that your pension may provide?
- What sort of financial provision will your pension make to your partner if you die?

Your loans

Think about how you are going to fund any loans that you
have. Will your pension be large enough to continue to make
the payments or should you try to pay extra while you are still
working? And what about anything large that you are going to
have to buy over the next months or years? You may want to
buy a new car, or need to replace the washing machine or tele-
vision. Is it worth trying to fund at least part of that from your
income now, rather than from your retirement pension?

Things to do:

- Work out carefully if you will manage to continue any
  repayments you have
- Work out if you could afford to pay extra now – and
  check there are no penalties for that
- Try to pay off expensive credit card balances. It may be
  worth your while using a fixed interest loan for this so
  that you reduce your monthly payments.

Warning: **If you use a loan to pay off credit card debt, be very
careful not to run up big bills on your plastic again.**

Things to think about:

- Will you need to replace any large items?
- How will you pay for them?
- Can you save now to avoid borrowing later?

Your tax

You will still be a taxpayer when your retire, if your income takes you above the tax threshold.

But you may find that your tax rate drops. Once your salary stops you may slip down from being a high-rate taxpayer to the ordinary rate, or even down to the 10% band. Keep an eye on your savings. Tax-free accounts won't be worth so much to you now.

If you and your partner pay tax at different rates, make sure that your savings are in the name of the person who pays it at the lower rate. You'll have less tax taken off the interest payments.

Expert tip: **If the interest from your savings is likely to nudge you up a tax band move some of your money into tax-free accounts such as National Savings certificates or a cash ISA.**

As you get older you get more tax breaks. Once you reach 65 (and it's the same age for men and women) you get an additional tax-free allowance, known as age allowance. This applies only to taxpayers whose annual income is below £17,000 (2000/01)

Personal allowances

Age under 65:	£4,385
Age 65–74:	£5,790
Age 75 and over:	£6,050

Need to know: **If your top tax rate is 10%, and the interest on your savings is being taxed before you get it, you can claim some of that tax back.**

Things to do:
- Check what tax rate you will be paying
- Move savings into your partner's name if they are on a lower tax rate
- Make sure you are not paying too much tax on your savings.

Things to think about:
- Are interest payments likely to push you up a tax band?
- Inheritance tax – if your assets, including your share of the house, are worth more than £234,000 (2000/01) think about doing some tax planning. See Chapter 7 for more details.

Checklist

- Have I checked that my savings are getting a decent rate of interest, and the accounts are still held in the most appropriate place?
- Will I want to pay off my mortgage?
- Does everyone who needs to, know the details of my retirement?
- Will I be able to afford the monthly payments on all the loans I have?
- If my partner or I will be paying less tax, have we made the right financial moves to take advantage of that?

9   Your house

⇨ **Your mortgage – is it ready to retire**
⇨ **Second homes – the pros and cons**
⇨ **Your property can make you money**

For many of us our house is our biggest asset. It's probably worth much more than we would ever have imagined. Various surges in house prices over the years have taken property values in many places sky high. And unlike your pension fund, the money you've sunk into your home is highly visible. A walk past any estate agent's window shows just how much you could sell for.

There will come a day, though it may not seem very likely at the moment, when your house suddenly transforms itself from being a drain on your income to an asset. The mortgage will be paid off so you won't be paying out hundreds of pounds every month. Better than that, you will be sitting on a property worth tens if not hundreds of thousands of pounds.

So spend a bit of time working out just what your bricks and mortar mean to you financially.

There are some decisions to take on:

- Your mortgage
- Investing in property.

Your mortgage

By your late 40s or early 50s you could well be nearing the end of your mortgage. You may not be quite there yet, but it's worth looking ahead to make sure everything is on course and the financial decisions you took years ago on your home loan are still sound. So what should you be doing with your mortgage? In part, it will depend on what sort of mortgage you have.

- Repayment
- Endowment
- Pension, PEP, ISA.

Repayment

With this type of mortgage, the amount you owe will have been going down over the years as you pay back capital. You may feel that you can afford to increase payments now so that you repay the whole loan much quicker. You will be paying more in interest to your mortgage lender than you are getting on any savings you have so it makes sound financial sense to do this. But remember, a mortgage is the cheapest form of borrowing there is so don't use up all your savings and have to take out a loan for other things. And watch out if you are on a fixed rate loan – there could be huge penalties for paying back the money early.

Cash saver: Be careful how you make extra payments. Check with your lender that any money you pay will be used to reduce your mortgage, and not held in a low-interest savings account for any length of time.

Endowment

Endowment mortgages have come in for a lot of criticism recently, as millions of borrowers have been receiving letters telling them that their endowment insurance plans may not grow by enough to pay off their mortgage. That means they could have a shortfall when their policy matures. The financial regulators are making the endowment providers write to all policyholders, giving them an idea of whether their policy is *expected* to pay off the loan.

Your letter may ask you to make higher payments to your policy, but you don't have to. There are several options available to make sure your mortgage is repaid.

You could consider:

- Switching part of your mortgage to a repayment basis
- Starting an ISA or savings account to build up an additional fund
- Paying off a part of your mortgage with a lump sum – if you have spare cash.

Talk to your financial adviser before you make a move.

Many people coming to the end of 20- or 25-year policies that they started in the 1970s are in a much better position. Not only will there be no shortfall, there ought to be a large surplus in their fund. Figures for 1999 show that the average 20-year with-profits endowment policy, set up to pay off a £50,000 mortgage, actually paid out almost £120,000 – that's £70,000 more than the target figure. That's a lot of holidays!

Pension, PEP, ISA mortgage

If you are saving in this sort of plan with a view to paying off your mortgage, keep an eye on values. Check, with a pension mortgage, that the amount you will take out as a cash sum to repay the loan looks likely to be large enough. Don't rely on your lender or pension provider to inform you automatically. They may not. If you have a PEP or ISA, and your money is invested in shares, work out the value of your portfolio or funds. If they are soaring away, you might think about cashing in part of the fund to repay a chunk of the loan. But take advice before making this move.

Investing in property

Your home will have almost certainly risen in value, possibly substantially, since you bought your first property. If your children have flown the nest, you may have more space on your hands than you need. Now could be a good time to invest in another property. You could trade down and use the capital from the family home to buy two smaller places, or you could take out a larger mortgage. The number of people who have bought second homes – either for pleasure or simply to make money – has risen dramatically over the years. It's not all plain sailing, but if you get it right, buying property can be a shrewd investment.

You could consider:

- Buying to let
- Buying a holiday home.

Buy to let

An increasing number of people are buying a second property as part of their pension planning, or simply to provide them with a steady income in later life. The idea is that you buy a flat or small house and rent it out so that the income you get is larger than the mortgage. If you don't have to take a loan, you'll make more money on it more quickly. An added bonus will be if the value of the property rises. Investing in property can seem like an easy way to make money, but don't be fooled. There are many pitfalls to catch out the unwary. Before you start looking at property, take advice from the experts. Talk to letting agents and anyone you know who has already bought a buy-to-let property. If you don't know anyone, ask agents to put you in touch with one of their clients.

Don't underestimate the amount of work you will have to do yourself. You can make money out of buy-to-let, but it's never easy money.

> *Expert tip:* **Imagine that for two months of every year you have no tenants and that rents drop by 20%. If you still think you can make money, you're probably right.**

Financing the deal

There are special mortgages you can use to finance buying a second property to rent out. These so-called buy-to-let mortgages will lend you money based on how much rent you will get, not on your income.

Buy-to-let mortgages:

- Usually only lend up to 80% of the property's value (some will lend 85%)
- Will expect the rent to be about ⅓ higher than the monthly mortgage
- Have a higher rate of interest than ordinary mortgages –

you can get good deals, but don't expect the lowest fixed or discounted rate.

Remember to add in the cost of insuring the property and its contents if you are letting it furnished.

Need to know: **Don't forget that you may have to pay capital gains tax (CGT) on some of the profit you make when you sell your property.**

Holiday homes

Many of us dream of owning a holiday home. A villa by the sea, an apartment in the mountains or a cottage in the country. And for an increasing number of people, that dream is becoming a reality. Don't underestimate the amount of money you could end up spending or it could all turn into a nightmare.

What you spend depends on what you can afford and where you buy. If you are looking abroad, you will have all sorts of unexpected extras. There will be fairly large continuing costs – such as service charges, insurance and utilities. And travelling costs every time you visit.

When buying abroad you should:

- Take expert advice from specialists in the UK. Contact FOPDAC (Federation of Overseas Property Developers, Agents and Consultants) on 020 8941 5588 or www.fopdac.com for a list of members
- Only buy in an area you know. At the very least you should have spent a couple of holidays in the town or village you are hoping to buy in

- Budget for the extras. Tax and legal fees can add at least 10% to property costs in many parts of Europe
- When you go and view properties, be in a position to do a deal there and then, but do not be pressurised into it
- Always use a local lawyer, don't just rely on the person who did the conveyancing on your UK home
- Watch out for currency changes. If the pound falls in value against the currency of the country in which you are buying, that will in effect put the price up
- Don't expect the property market to go up and down as sharply as it can in the UK.

Expert tip: **Although mortgage rates on continental Europe are lower than in the UK, the amount you can borrow is also lower – 80% of the property's value is the maximum – most people borrow 60–70%.**

Final word

You don't have to take major decisions on your home in a rush. But spend some time thinking about the options. Your house may provide you with an income that you didn't expect and that may make all the difference to your lifestyle when you retire.

10 Taking your pension

⇨ **Your state pension: how and when to claim**
⇨ **The lump sum – is cash up-front the right option**
⇨ **Understanding annuities, the jargon you have to learn**

It's decision time again. Having made it to retirement your money plans suddenly switch. Instead of paying into your pension every month – it's about to start paying you money.

But you have to choose how you want that money paid. Some of your colleagues who've already retired will no doubt tell you the merits of opting for a lump sum; others will have chosen to have a larger pension income. Don't just follow in the path of someone else. Make sure that you are making the right decisions for your financial circumstances. You should take advice from a professional – but before you do that, read on. Spend a little time making sure you understand what's involved. It's not difficult and you won't be able to judge the advice you're getting unless you know what the terms mean.

First things first. Make sure that you're getting all the payments that you're entitled to.

Over the years you could have paid into:

• Your basic state pension, through National Insurance
• SERPs – the State Earnings Related Pensions scheme
• A company pension
• A personal pension
• Pension top-ups.

State pension

When you reach retirement age – 65 for men or 60 for women, (although that is changing from 2010) – you are entitled to receive your state pension, provided you have contributed enough in National Insurance payments throughout your working life. Currently (2000/01) the full state pension is £67.50 a week for a single person and £107.90 for married couples. From 6th April 2001, the figures will be £72.50 for a single pensioner and £115.90 for a couple.

Need to know: **Women who reach 60 after the year 2010 won't qualify for a state pension on their 60th birthday. Over the course of the next decade, women are being brought into line with men so that by 2020 everyone will be eligible for their state pension at 65.**

How to claim it

Four months before you reach state retirement age, you should receive a letter from the DSS with a form telling you how to claim your pension. If you haven't received one three months before you reach retirement age, you should contact your local Benefits Agency office (their number will be in the business pages of the phone book or Yellow Pages under Government Offices). If you don't claim your pension when you retire, you can only get it backdated for up to three months.

> *Need to know:* **You don't have to take your pension when you reach state retirement age – you can put it off and get pension increments instead. This means that when you finally do take your state pension, it will be at a higher rate.**

SERPs

The state earnings related pension (SERPs) will only be part of your pension package if you have paid into it. It's an add-on to your state pension and is paid at the same time.

Company pension scheme

If you've paid into a pension scheme set up by your employer, you will be entitled to a payout when you retire. How you will be paid depends on the type of scheme you are a member of.

Final salary scheme

Your pension will be calculated as a percentage of your final salary. See Chapter 3 for full details of how these schemes work.

How to claim it

About 3–6 months before you retire you'll be given information about how you can take your pension. Some large employers run a series of pre-retirement courses for workers; others will just spell out your options in a letter.

You can:

- Take all your pension as a monthly income

- Or opt for a tax-free cash lump sum and a smaller income.

Full details on which is the best option for you come later in this chapter.

Cash caution: **Don't forget that all your pensions, including the state pension, are taxable. If your taxable income is more than £5,790 (2000/01) for anyone aged between 65 and 74, or £6,050 for 75 and over, you will have to pay tax.**

Money purchase scheme
Your pension will depend on how many years you have been a member of the scheme, and how much you and your employer have been paying in. It will also be affected by the investments that your money has been in.

How to claim it
Your employer has to write to you six months before you retire telling you what your options are. And again you can choose to take part of your pension as a tax-free lump sum. You will be told the maximum you can take as a lump sum and what the effect will be on the fund that's left over. As it is still an occupational pension scheme, there can be a number of rules on how you buy your annuity (that's the correct name for what we generally call a pension – an income for life). Your scheme may insist you buy a spouse's pension, or that you have to ensure your income will rise in line with inflation. Some schemes will search for the best annuity on your behalf; others will leave the hard work to you (see below).

Group personal pension

The amount you have in your pension fund will depend on how much you have been paying into the scheme and the investment performance of the fund.

How to claim it

Although this pension is offered by your employer, it's not an occupational scheme, so don't expect a letter from your company. Instead, your pension provider will contact you around three months before you retire. You will be told the value of your fund, where it is invested and given an idea of how much of a monthly income that would buy you.

Need to know: You may not know what kind of pension you are in when you retire – occupational or personal. Your first starting point is your employer – contact the pensions or human resources departments. Failing that, try the pension company whose name appears on any correspondence you have.

Personal pension plan

Your pension will depend on how much you have been paying into it, and the investment performance of the fund.

How to claim it

As with group personal pensions, you should be contacted directly by your pension provider and given a choice about how you take your pension.

Pension top-ups

You may have been boosting your pension by paying into other schemes such as AVCs and FSAVCs (see Chapter 3 for full details) or by buying added years through a final salary scheme.

How to claim it

You can be flexible about when you take your AVCs. They don't have to be paid alongside your other pensions. Check your scheme rules. Added years must be paid along with your final salary pension.

What are the options?

One of the most important decisions you will have to make is how you want to take your pension. Do you want a tax-free lump sum?

You'll be asked whether you want to take your pension:

- As a monthly income only
- As a smaller monthly income and cash lump sum.

Monthly income only

This means that your fund will buy an annuity (that's the technical term for what you would call your pension), which will give you a monthly income for the rest of your life. When you die your pension will die with you – unless you have made arrangements for it to continue for the life of your spouse.

Smaller income and cash lump sum

This means you get a tax-free lump sum in your hand, and a

smaller monthly income. When you die, the pension dies with you (unless the life of your spouse is covered too) but what's left of your lump sum will be there to be used by your heirs.

Need to know: **You can use any lump sum that you take to buy an annuity and so increase your monthly income.**

Most people go for as large a tax-free lump sum as they can. But it isn't always the best option. It all comes down to your individual circumstances, so what's right for a colleague may not be right for you.

The cash lump sum option gives you:

- Flexibility – if you need cash up-front to pay off your mortgage or buy a new car. Or you can simply invest it in a different type of policy – to spread your risk
- Tax efficiency – the money is tax-free and can then be invested in tax-efficient savings plans, such as an ISA
- Control – when you die the lump sum, or what's left of it, does not disappear.

The full pension option gives you:

- Certainty – you will have a larger monthly income
- Discipline – you won't be tempted to spend the lump sum that should be used for adding to your income
- Simplicity – you don't have to worry about investing the cash.

> *Cash saver:* If your spouse is a non-taxpayer, you could trans-
> fer your tax-fee lump sum into their name. That way you
> won't be taxed on the income from it.

Buying your pension

You have to use part of the pension fund you have built up to
provide you with a regular income for the rest of your life. It's
usually a monthly income, and this pension is technically
known as an annuity. You don't have to buy your annuity immediately, but you do have to take the plunge at the very
latest by your 75th birthday.

The income that you get depends on what are known as
annuity rates, and sadly these rates (along with interest rates
in general) have been going down over the last few years.

This means that the same size pension pot buys a smaller
income.

For a 65-year-old man:
- In 1990 a £100,000 fund bought an annual income of
  around £15,000
- In 2000 a £100,000 fund bought an annual income of
  around £9,000.

The good news though, is that with a bit of careful shopping around, you can make your money go further.

Shop for your annuity.

'Shopping around' is such a cliché when it comes to getting a
good deal, but it is really worth your while with annuities.

You can buy your annuity from any provider (usually an insurance company) you like – you don't have to stick with the company that your pension is with. And it's possible to bump up your income by 15% by getting the best deal. It's difficult to compare rates yourself. You will have to go to an annuity specialist or financial adviser. Annuity rates change daily as it is a volatile market – so you need to see someone who has up-to-the-minute access to the best rates.

If you are not in the best of health or you smoke, make sure your annuity provider knows this. You should get more money because, putting it bluntly, you aren't expected to live as long as people in good health. The annual income you get from your lump sum is calculated using complicated tables. But how long you are expected to live is one of the main factors taken into consideration. So anyone with a shortened life expectancy will get a higher income.

Expert tip: **Take professional advice before you choose your annuity provider. Once you've decided, there's no going back.**

Other retirement choices

There are other factors to think about when you're buying your annuity. Ask yourself:
- Do I want an income for my spouse after I die?
- Do I want my pension to rise in line with inflation?
- Am I prepared to take a risk with my annuity?

Single or joint?

You can use your pension fund to buy an income not only for yourself, but one that will carry on and make payments to your spouse after you die. It does mean that you will get less while you are alive. But it is well worth thinking about. Traditionally, husbands are the main breadwinners and therefore most likely to have a large pension fund. Sadly, they are also likely to be outlived by their wives. So if a husband takes out an annuity that will just provide an income for him (a single life annuity), his wife will receive nothing when he dies.

It doesn't have to be an all or nothing option – you may both decide that if the wife was left on her own, she would only need 50% of the pension, or perhaps even less than that. It may be that she might sell the home and move somewhere much smaller, perhaps into a flat, and use some of the money released from the property to fund her old age. Think it through carefully before you decide and, whatever you do, make sure you discuss your pension options together.

Inflation-proofed pension

Most of us haven't yet got used to the fact that we're living for much longer. Anyone retiring at 60 could have to support themselves for another 20 or 25 years. And early retirement could bump that figure up to as much as 30 years. Although inflation is running at low levels at the moment, many of us can remember when it was much higher.

Cash caution: Even if inflation stays at low levels for the next 20 years, it will eat away at your pension. An inflation rate of just 2½% will reduce the buying power of £1,000 to a little over £600. At 5%, the £1,000 reduces to a mere £370.

You can choose an annuity that rises every year and that way try to maintain the buying power of your pension. You can pick a percentage for yourself, say 3% or 5%, or you can link your pension payments directly to the rate of inflation. It does mean that the amount you get at the beginning will be lower, but as you get older you won't find your pension shrinking away.

Need to know: Many pensioners find that their pension is at its lowest in their final years when they need the money most. Often they have to pay for extras such as more heating or help around the house. Having a flat-rate pension could be a false economy.

Taking a risk with your annuity

With annuity rates at historically low levels, many pensioners are trying to find ways of boosting their retirement income – even if it means taking a bit of a risk. You can buy investment-linked annuities, which invest part or all of the fund in the stockmarket. There are two options:

- With-profits
- Unit-linked.

A with-profits annuity is the lower risk of the two options. Your money is invested in shares, but also in property and government-backed bonds (gilts). It means that the performance you get from your fund should be much smoother – and you ought to be shielded from some of the ups and downs of the stockmarket.

A unit-linked fund means that you are tied directly to the fortunes of the stockmarket. You may find it unnerving for your pension fund to increase and decrease on a weekly basis. If that's the case you could split your fund and just invest part of it in a unit-linked annuity, or not invest in a unit-linked fund at all.

Home truth: **You may feel that retirement is the time when you can't afford to take financial risks with your money. If that's the case, choose a safer option. There's no point chasing that extra buck if it means you can't sleep at night.**

Income drawdown

There is one last term that it's worth understanding if you have a large pension fund. And that's income drawdown – an option for anyone with a fund of least £200,000, or possibly more.

You use a formalised scheme to take a regular income from your pension fund, and delay buying an annuity. Your fund is invested, usually in shares, until you finally buy an annuity (which you must do no later than your 75th birthday). It should make enough money for you to get an income that's the same or even higher than you would have got from an annuity. Most people who go for this income drawdown option hope that rates will have risen by the time they come to buying their annuity. But there are no guarantees – indeed, annuity rates could fall further.

There are advantages to income drawdown:

- When you buy your annuity you will be older and so should get higher payments
- If you die, your fund doesn't disappear
- You can vary the amounts of income you take and so cut your tax bill.

And the disadvantage? Any money that you spend won't be there to pay into the annuity when the time comes.

You are taking a risk with your pension fund. And there is no guarantee that annuity rates will be any better when you come to buy yours. Many financial advisers recommend income drawdown only if you have money coming in from other sources – possibly another pension or rental income from a house or flat.

If you have several pensions to take – perhaps because you moved jobs or are self-employed – you could take them at different times. They don't all have to click in together.

Expert tip: **Income drawdown is a complicated area. You must take advice from a professional before you go down this route. Make sure they have explained all the risks and the costs involved to you fully, otherwise you could be in for a nasty shock.**

Putting your feet up

⇨ **Balance your cash with your spending**
⇨ **Retire – then go back to work**

The time has come. The early morning alarm has gone off for the last time and you have retired. It may be a welcome release from the drudgery of work; perhaps you feel your useful days are over; or maybe your retirement is unexpected, something that's happened because of ill-health or redundancy.

Whatever the reason, retirement will make a major change to your lifestyle. You may have less money coming in but you'll have a lot more of something else – time. And using that time could make you quids in. You'll be able to travel off-peak, take advantage of plenty of cut-price offers, and spend some of your time looking for bargains.

Having invested money for your retirement throughout your life, it's now worth spending a little time thinking through what lies ahead so that you make all the right moves.

Home truth: **Always talk through your plans with your partner to make sure that they agree with what you're about to do.**

Check through these areas:

- Your spending plans – are they in line with your income?
- Work after work – part-time, voluntary or set up alone
- Getting financial help
- How to get the best deals.

Your spending plans

First things first. Make sure you know what income you have – and where it's coming from. In the past most of your money will have come from your work – probably as a monthly salary payment directly into your bank. Now you might have bits and pieces coming from various sources. And the money won't all be paid monthly so it's important to know the date you expect the payment. Fill in the table below so that you know exactly how much you will have.

Source	How much	When
Main pension		
Other pensions		
State pension		
Interest from savings		
Income from investments		
Part-time work		
Anything else		

Now you have to work out whether you will be spending less than you have coming in. Or do you need a top-up? You may be able to use any lump sum you have – perhaps from your pension, savings or investments – to generate income. See Chapter 10 for more details.

Or there may come a time when you have to spend some of your capital. Many pensioners steer clear of doing this for fear of running out of money. Try to take a middle course. There's no point in scrimping and saving throughout your retirement, and then leaving a large lump sum in your will.

But make a note in your diary to check your spending every three months for the first year. By then you should be in control.

Expert tip: **Keep all paperwork. Letters and documents should be filed away. You may not need them now, but you just might in the future, so it's worth filling a lever arch file rather than a waste bin.**

An added bonus of giving up work is the financial savings that you might not have thought of. Household insurance bills can be cut – many insurance companies charge less if you don't regularly leave the house unoccupied all day; there will be no travel to work costs; you won't need to buy clothes for work, or contribute to leaving and wedding presents. But you will almost certainly spend more on heating.

Work after work

You may not want to give up altogether once you jack in the day job. There are lots of options open to you.

You may want to:
- Work part-time
- Do voluntary work

- Start up your own business.

Work part-time
You can do as much, or as little, work as you like and it won't affect your pension. But you will probably have to pay tax on your earnings. What you earn will be added to all the other income you have and you will be taxed accordingly. If the tax is not taken off your money before you get it, you will have to fill in a self-assessment form. The Inland Revenue doesn't always send you a form automatically, so you may have to write and ask for one. Don't just hope it will all go away, it won't, and putting it off will make matters worse.

Cash caution: **Pensioners who are over 65 and who have more than £17,000 a year (2000/01) coming in, will start to lose the extra tax break they get – the Age Allowance. So if you are on the threshold, it may be worth your while to cut down your hours. You won't lose the whole Age Allowance at a stroke. But it is clawed back very quickly and gives the impression of pushing up your tax rate. Try to avoid this.**

Do voluntary work
You might want to get involved in non-paying work just to keep your brain active, and to put something back into society.

You won't get paid for any of this work – though you sometimes get help with some of your expenses – but you should get a great deal of satisfaction.

Start up your own business

You may have a hobby that you are now hoping to make some cash from; or you might want to take the plunge and really try your hand at being your own boss and go into business. Many people do very well financially, have a lot of fun and end up with a business they can pass on to their children. Many more lose a lot of money trying something they just couldn't cope with.

If you start small, you will limit your losses. But remember if you are running your operation from home, tell your insurance company about it. You'll want any special equipment covered by your insurance policy and they'll want to know if you are increasing the risk.

Expert tip: **You might find your insurance premiums go up, but it's better to pay a bit more than lose the cover altogether.**

Starting a larger business, which involves renting premises and hiring staff, will require more help. There are legal, employment and trading regulations you have to be aware of, but there are plenty of organisations that can guide you through. Try these websites: www.fsb.org.uk or www.dti.gov.uk.

You may want to do something as simple as a bit of light gardening, cake decoration, or even house sitting. Don't be tempted to join the black economy. The Inland Revenue is tightening up on people who try to avoid paying tax on their earnings. If you're not earning much you won't have to pay much tax, but you'll be vastly out of pocket if you get caught with an undeclared income and have to pay a large fine.

Getting financial help

If you can't manage on your income, and you don't have a nest egg to help you along, don't panic. There's help available. The government does have a safety net in the form of the Benefits Agency and there are plenty of benefits that you can apply for. Don't be put off. You've been making National Insurance contributions all your working life – it's your financial right to take the benefits when you need them.

Many of the benefits are means tested – you will only get help if:

- You are on a low income
- Have very little in the way of savings.

But always apply – they can only turn you down. Try the DSS Public Enquiry Office on 020 7712 2171, or use the website www.dss.gov.uk.

How to get the best deals

No matter what you are buying now, shop around. For once you should have the time to get quotes from several sources.

- Use the experts – brokers, agents, advisers – who should have access to cheaper deals than you might get yourself
- Let your fingers do the walking – phone around to check prices and see where the cheapest deals are
- Trawl the internet – if you are connected to the web, log on and search for yourself
- Ask your friends – if they've done some research you could piggy back on to it
- Don't be above a bit of bartering – you can sometimes get an extra discount just by asking for it

Top ten tips

- Don't save up to die. Spend some of your hard-earned cash and enjoy life.

- Plan ahead. No matter how off course your pension plans are, you can only do something about it if you know what you've got.

- Having a pension is not enough. Putting away £20 a month won't fund a luxurious old age.

- A decent pension later in life may mean cutbacks now – it's a choice you'll have to make.

- Remember you may have more than you think. Moving somewhere smaller will release cash.

- Don't ignore tax breaks – you'll be quids in.

- Keep tight control over your cash when you first retire. You can relax a little once you know where you stand financially.

- Prepare yourself mentally for life after work. Plan how you are going to fill your days.

- Don't forget to spend some of your money on yourself – you've earned it.

- Encourage your children to think about pensions early, so that their retirement will be comfortable.

And finally

Don't forget there's more to retirement than financial planning. Don't cut a corner too many and find that you could be having a much better time if you weren't wheeling and dealing and cost cutting quite so much. You're heading for your golden years. Enjoy them.

Acknowledgements

I am very grateful for the considerable amount of help I have had from Lloyds TSB in checking the detail of this book. I am particularly indebted to John Chettoe, Hardeep Sidhu, Stewart Redpath and Michael Huke for the time and trouble they have taken with the project. I am grateful to my brother George Mitchell and, as always, special thanks to my friend and colleague at the BBC, Sarah Pennells.

Alison Mitchell, *January 2001*